WONDERFUL Butterflies and Mandalas COLORING BOOK

Designs for Relaxation and Mindfulness

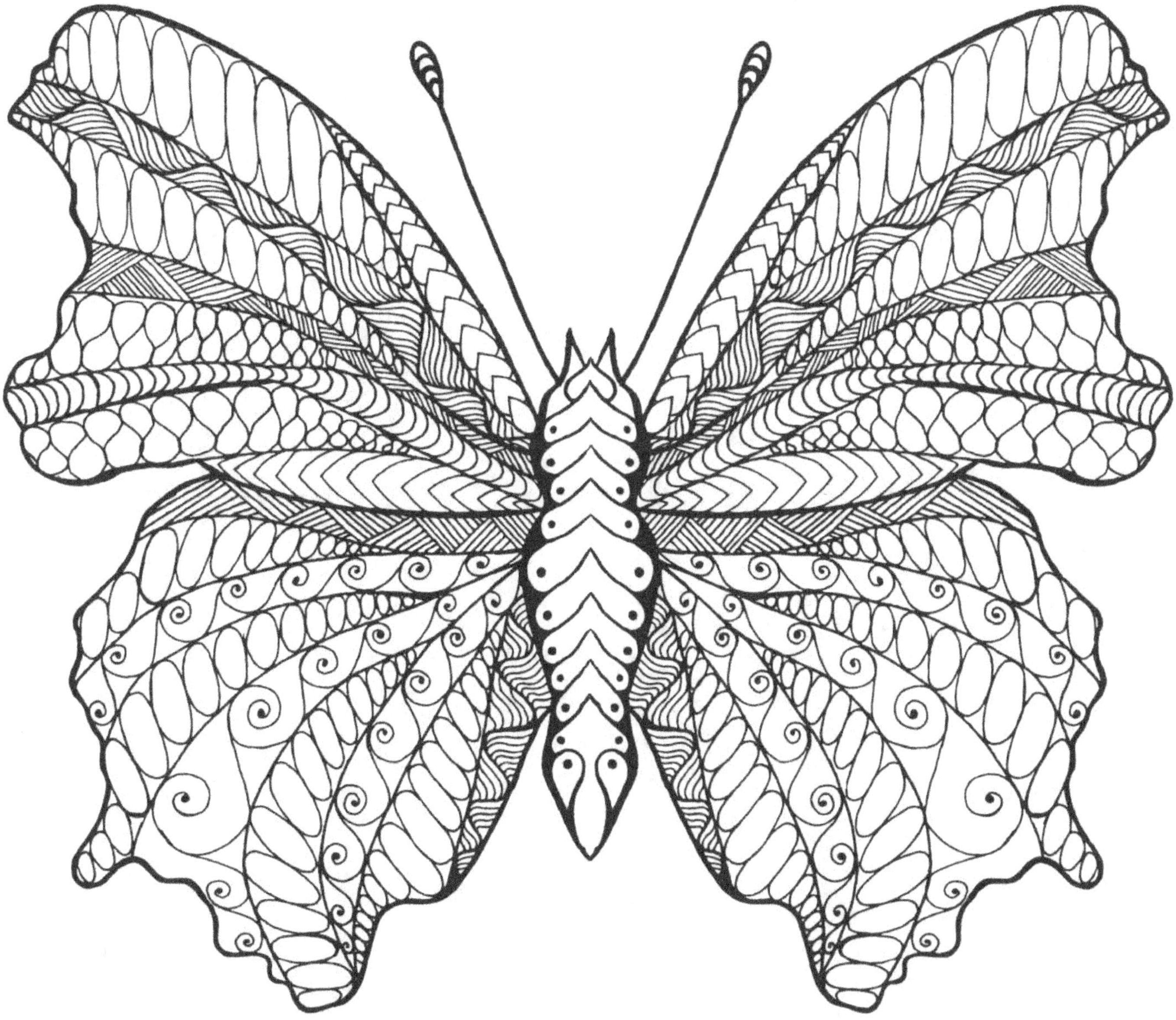

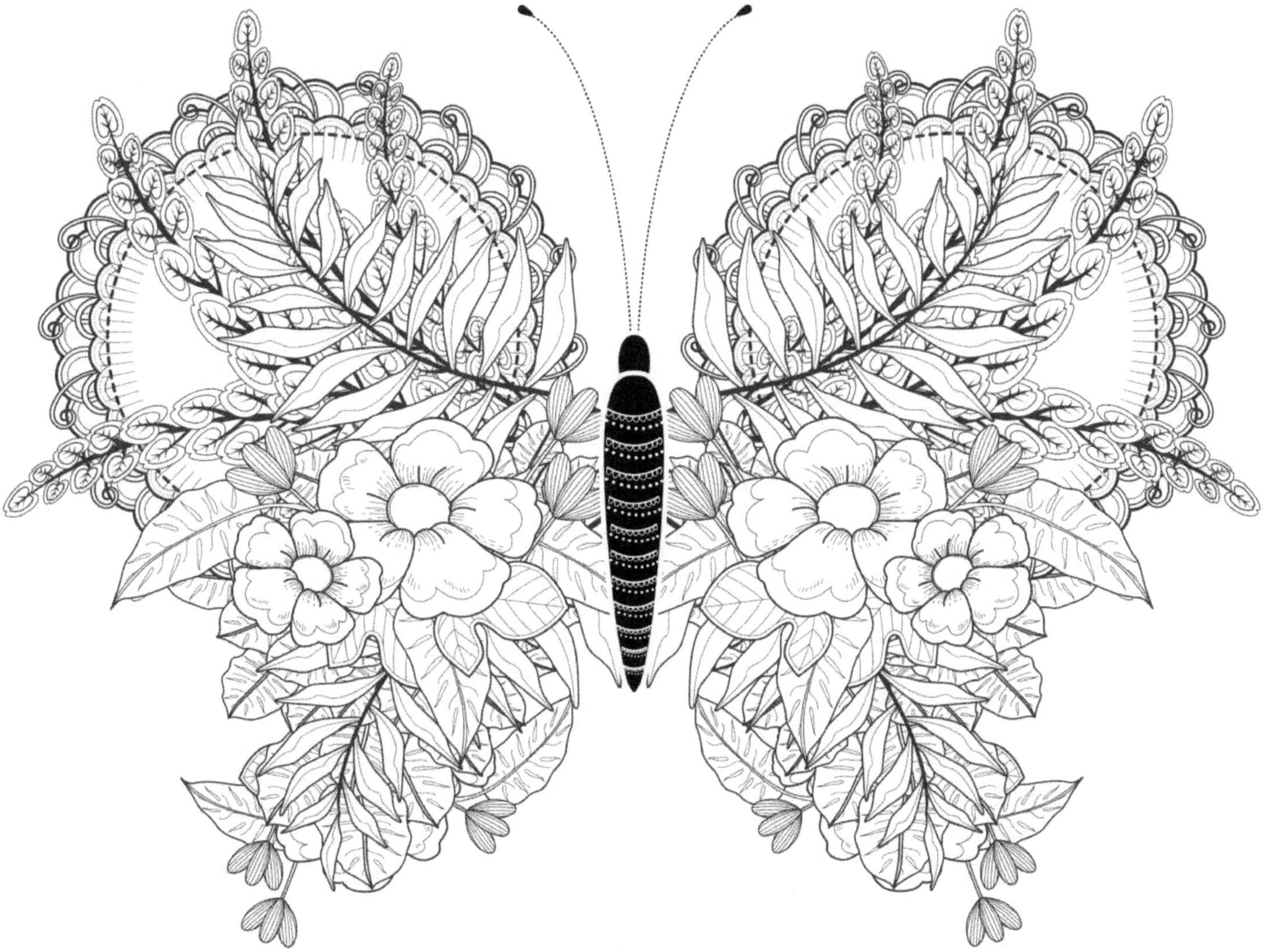

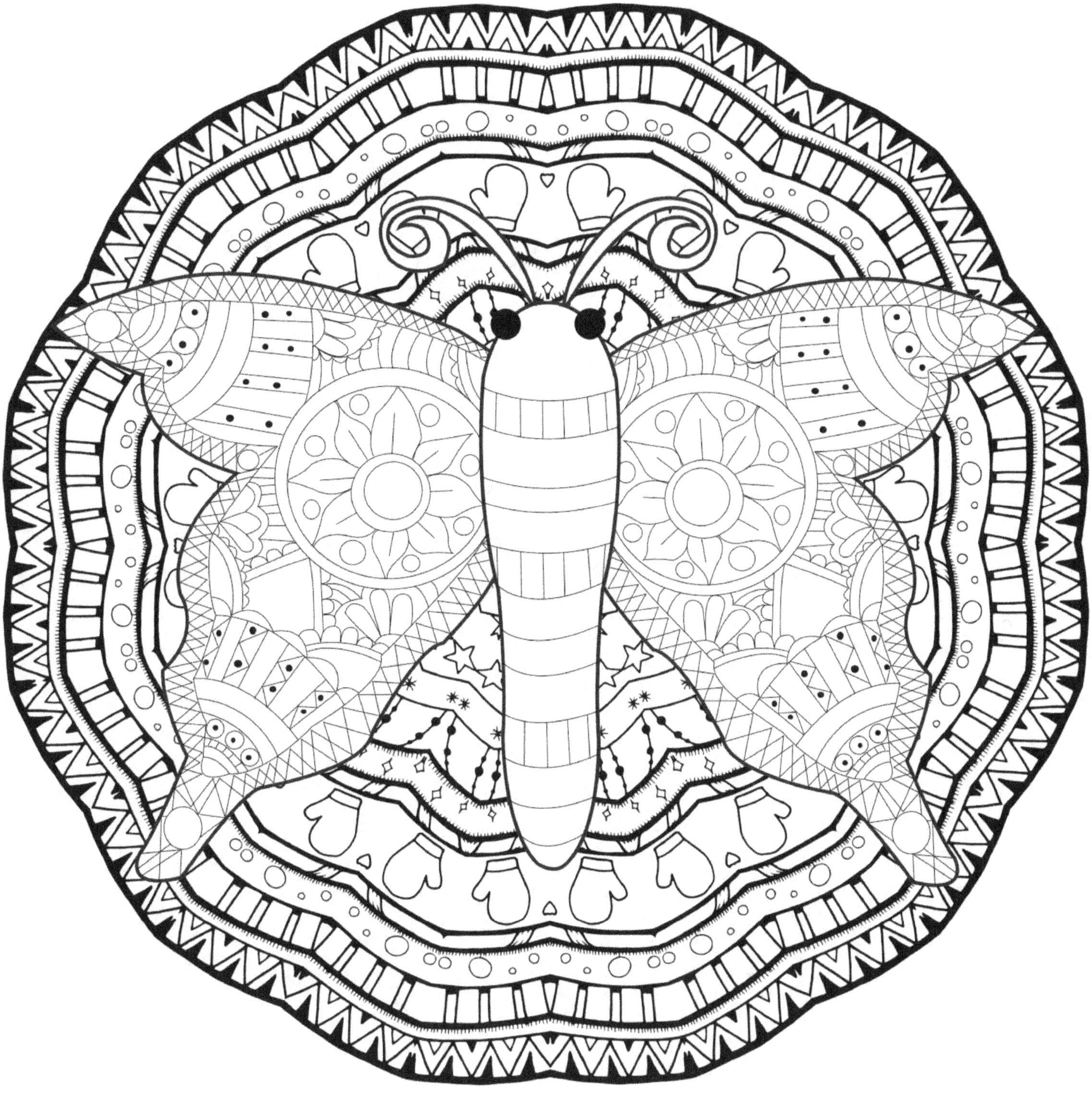

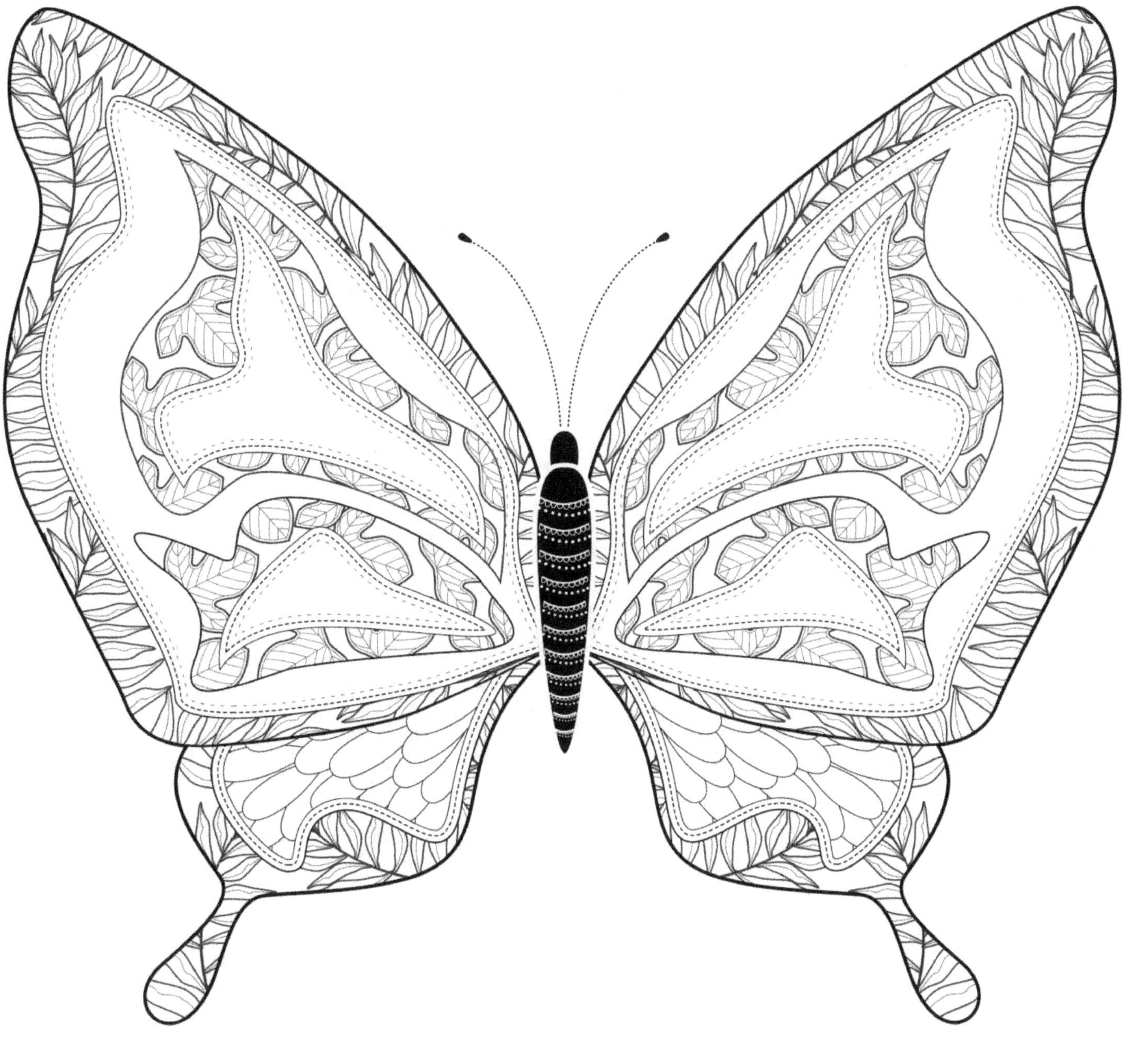

www.ingramcontent.com/pod-product-compliance
Lightning Source LLC
Chambersburg PA
CBHW081155280526
45787CB00008B/3332
9781547245253